THE GRADUATE'S COMPANION

THE GRADUATE'S COMPANION

7 Vital Questions To
Answer Before Graduation

Marricke Kofi Gane

Contents

DEDICATION

This book is dedicated to my grandma, Comfort Nyonyoh
– who made my years in school a very comfortable one.
I love you.

INTRODUCTION

My name is Marricke Kofi Gane. I am a professional accountant, an author and an International Development expert.

My purpose for writing this book is to raise some questions for your consideration before you migrate from the world of tertiary school into what many have called the "real world". These are very interesting questions which do not relate to your final exams, but ones that will make your entire time spent at university or other tertiary institution, very worthwhile in terms of the impact you can make in the world on graduation. There is a very high possibility these are not the usual types of questions you may have been asked all through your educational journey, until now.

Years ago, I was a student just like you, sitting in a lecture room and trying to earn a university or professional qualification. If you are in that position at the time of reading this book, I want to congratulate you for a job well done, irrespective of what stage you are on your learning journey. The journey is what matters most – it gives you the needed rigour, focus, discipline and preparation for what lies ahead in life after campus. Believe you me, you will be needing all of that for the rest of your life. Congratulations once again.

Within a few days, weeks or years from now, you will

be completing your tertiary education and entering into the "real world". For some of you, it will be your first experience of the world outside of campus and, for others, you are returning to the world of work. Whatever the case may be, know this - there is a world waiting out there for you. It does not matter whether that world is going to require you to get a job or to establish a new business. It might even involve travelling to explore the world or going on to further studies – whatever it is, there is still a world out there and you need to be prepared to face it. This is where this book comes in useful, as it will present you with some of the hard facts you need to know as well as some of the tough questions you need to answer in that preparatory process.

I am certain it will add something to you.

PUTTING IT IN PERSPECTIVE

For a moment, I would like you to compare your time at university to a woman carrying a new pregnancy. Over the next nine months, the mother will provide all the nutrients needed for this child to develop its brain, digestive and nervous systems as well as its five senses, among other things. Then, one day, that baby is born into the world and he has to breathe with his own lungs, eat with his own mouth and fight diseases with his own immune system in order to survive. The survival of this child will depend largely on whether or not he was fully and properly developed in the womb before birth.

In the same manner, your journey through tertiary education is just like the baby's. You have spent a period of time in school trying to build the knowledge foundation for your future success. Your tertiary school environment is like the womb in which you are growing intellectually and in other ways, in preparation for delivery into the real world. Your wonderful lecturers are the veins and blood vessels that supply you with the nutrients you need to grow and develop in maturity, discipline, knowledge and wisdom. Then comes the day when you graduate and are "born into the world" outside of academia.

This is a day you all look forward to and it will surely come. So the important question you need to ask at this time is - how will I survive in that big world waiting outside? This book is designed to help you answer this most crucial question.

HERE'S YOUR REALITY CHECK – AND IT'S FREE

People who leave tertiary school usually end up facing one of the following scenarios:

1. Being employed by a company or an individual – the majority tend to do this;
2. Setting up their own business - although not many travel this route;
3. Leaving their town or country altogether to look for employment in greener pastures;
4. Undertaking additional studies like masters or doctoral degree or some other study;
5. Feeling so overwhelmed by the realities of their new world, that they surrender to their so-called fate, give up on their dreams, settle for the ordinary or resign themselves to doing nothing.

Whichever path you choose, there are a few hard facts you need to know – a kind of reality check, if you wish. The intent is not to scare you, but to help you get smartened to manoeuvre yourself through the many wonderful as well as challenging mazes of the real world. So, do keep in mind the following:

- For those of you intending to get employed, you should know that unemployment rates are still running along and you are not the only one looking for a job. So temper your expectations. If it happens quickly, consider it your good fortune, be very grateful for this break and give it your best effort. Bear in mind that every day there are hundreds unemployed persons ready to step into your shoes if you falter.

- For those who want to go into business as entrepreneurs, remember that the competition in the business world is ruthless and that you will be the small fish swimming in the same ocean as sharks and whales – at least for starters. In this world, there is no such thing as a free lunch – everything has a price, except integrity. Remember this and always capitalize on your strengths. Naivety could kill you and your business if you are not the type who has the discipline, perseverance and the willingness to know all you can about an area business, experience setbacks and still press on to the end irrespective. Without such a mind-set, you might be setting yourself up to crash. If you asked my advice about the best tools for success in business, my reply would be, unreservedly, your creativity and your resolve.

- For those who wish to go searching for greener pastures, you most definitely might enjoy the flight but only you will know if you have found a greener patch. What I would like to tell you however, is that the grass grows green wherever in the world you find it, as long as it gets the water, sunshine and fertile ground it needs. For many people, going away is sometimes simply an excuse to run away from working hard on their own lot until they find gold. The real question you need to ask yourself is - what is the motivation for leaving? Have you taken enough time to explore the opportunities where you are before going off abroad? Have you considered what advantages you have in your present environment that you might not have elsewhere in your anticipated greener pastures? Oh, and remember, you are not likely to be the only one seeing that place as a greener pasture. More than likely, others do too and so when you get there, you just might have to fight for your own spot.

- For those seeking to do additional studies, you need to ask: what exactly are you going to study and why? Advanced degrees or professional qualifications might give you something extra to offer your employers, but just doing these courses for the sake of doing them does not necessarily boost your employability. The truth is,

employers are not always looking for additional qualifications, instead, they are always looking out for people
who have some value to add to their business. So until
your education can deliver some value and competitive
edge to an employer, do not be fooled into believing
those qualifications by themselves are enough to get you
a job. Any employer will find it hard to justify the need to
pay you a very high salary because of your qualifications
but without a corresponding high value added return on
his investment.

- For this reason, serious thought should be given to
undertaking further studies. It should not be done just
to while away the time caused by unemployment, but
rather to gain some lifelong learning from it. Personally,
I feel that before undertaking something like a master's
degree, you will greatly benefit if you first worked in
the related field to gain some insights into the practical
areas of your course. This should provide you with many
valuable insights as you have an opportunity to interro-
gate the theory of the course by putting it into practical
perspective.

- And finally, for those of you who want to surrender to
what you see as your fate and give up your dreams and

settle for less or nothing at all, I would like to say this; remember the number of years you spent at college or university educating yourself. Can you give all this up that easily? Then, maybe you should not have started the journey at all. With all that investment in yourself, this is no time to withdraw from the race. Nothing good comes easily and certainly an opportunity to fulfil your dreams and achieve your destiny is worth fighting for. Believe me; not trying at all is a far greater waste of a person's life than trying something and failing.

Please do not get me wrong. None of what I am saying is to discourage you from getting a job, starting your own business, travelling to other places to work, pursuing higher studies or even doing nothing, if this is what you wish. In fact, all I am saying is that there are some realities you need to face, depending on which path you choose to follow after leaving school.

At this point, I want to make two statements that I need you to remember for the remainder of your time in tertiary education – it is also valid if you have just graduated recently.

The world is changing and it is doing so at a very rapid rate and this is not likely to stop anytime soon. It is speeding along like a very fast train which, if stopped abruptly, would cause severe accidents. The world, as it is presently, will continue to grow in three main directions – speed, creativity and integration. I say this because:

1. Prior to the information age, it used to be that those with money and natural resources had a lot of power. Today, the people demonstrating considerable financial and social power are those with the knowledge, information and the creativity to turn such knowledge and information into something the world needs.

2. Before the age of technology, it was individuals with experience that had superiority in the work place. Today, these experiences can be gained without one having to live through them and so creativity is beginning to trump experience.

3. Years ago, the world was full of all sorts of barriers to communication. Today, through the convergence of information technology and telecommunications, the whole world has become a global village in which almost everyone can be instantly connected to another person in any part of the world by using a simple mobile phone.

Ladies and gentlemen, if you are reading this, I very humbly submit to you, that we are in the new era resulting from a fusion of "creativity, information, global access and knowledge" (CIGAK). This is the real world awaiting you in our century.

That is why people like you should be winners. You must not fail. In fact, you do not have an excuse to fail after a tertiary education, even though every day unemployment is rising, economies are failing or shrinking, and the world is ever changing. Despite all these things, you are living in one of the most creative periods in human history, facilitated largely through the wide availability of technology to stimulate the imagination and turn your visions into reality. It is now easier more than it has ever been to creatively use your personal knowledge to provide innovative solutions that the world needs and which can bring you great success. By employing technology in every area of enterprise, you can greatly reduce the gap between knowledge, ideas and product development to quickly satisfy consumer needs. In addition, modern technology allows you to reach billions of people with whatever unique products you have to offer to the world.

I am sure you have heard the saying – "knowledge is power" – but the truth is that knowledge by itself is only potential power. It only becomes real power when it is used to create the kind of life you want for yourself and others. Otherwise, knowledge is indeed powerless.

AND NOW, THE QUESTIONS

1. *Who Owns Your Knowledge: Yourself Or Someone Else?*

I know before you finish reading this question, you will chuckle and say to yourselves *"me of course – I own my knowledge."* But here's the catch - what you do with the knowledge you have received in your respective tertiary institutions on graduating will determine if you went through all these years of hard work acquiring knowledge for yourself or for someone else.

If your knowledge is adding more value in quality and monetary terms to someone else or an organisation than yourself, then it really doesn't matter if you are being paid a salary – they own your knowledge. Yes, your brain is still yours because it physically sits in your head, but they own the knowledge you have in it. Simply put, the one who derives the most value from your knowledge is indeed the one who owns your knowledge. By extension therefore, they also own the many years you spent in school to acquire that knowledge.

Having said that, let me add this: that if you need to work to build a set of practical skills or experience, then by all means find a job and work, but do not end up being a slave to a job. If it turns out that the job is one that you love and being in it eventually makes you develop your strengths and abilities; if the job proportionately rewards you with a substantive value for your input now or in the future, then stay in it. However, if this is not the case, get whatever learning you need and move on. By thinking in this manner, the job serves you instead of you being its slave.

The whole reason for making this point is that you will leave school with a certain mind-set on how to approach the job market. What I would not recommend is for you to go into the job market with the idea that it is the final destination after all your years of studying. However, this could still be a possibility if you find yourself working in a field you enjoy which rewards you with equal or more value than it takes from you. Otherwise, seeing your job as an end could bring you to a place where if you no longer have the job, you could feel that the world has been taken away from you. However, if you see your job as a means to an end, then if it doesn't work out, you would only need to reassess the situation and think of a new way of getting to your life's goal.

In many cultures of the world, young people are still being told: *"go to school, study hard, get a job and it will guarantee you security in life and make you successful"*. Well, this no longer holds true, and if you leave school with this mind-set, you are likely to feel like a failure if you don't get a job. This might cause you to never think of applying your knowledge elsewhere. Perhaps, now is a good time to sound a warning about allowing your creativity to be bound by your job. This is very likely to happen in the circumstance where you see a job as the final destination or as a culmination point for all your academic efforts. This kind of thinking blinds you from finding reason to apply your knowledge elsewhere, other than on your job. This becomes the very limitation that prevents you from expanding your vision and can lead to you disregarding the value of all the knowledge you have acquired to date other than what you'll need to get by in a job.

Just remember that knowledge cannot be confined – and as such, if you ever find yourself in a situation where it feels like your knowledge can only be utilized on a job and nowhere else, then you have sold off your intellectual birth right to your employers. It is important for you to realize that the argument about others owning your knowledge is a reality, and that it results primarily from you deciding to confine the application of your acquired knowledge exclusively to your employer's work. This is a choice nobody else but you can make. Don't.

2. *Where Exactly Are You Going?*

In my first ever authored book, I presented a story for which the moral was that knowing your destination and what you will be doing when you get there determines everything else. I used an example of two brothers on separate journeys. One brother was headed for the north-pole where it is extremely cold and the other was going to the extremely hot desert of Morocco. Both of them were attending weddings. Now, it is obvious that although they were departing from the same country and attending the same kind of event, because their destinations were different, they would do a lot of things differently. These differences would affect the type of food they ate, the clothing they wore and the transportation they used, among other things – all determined by their destinations.

The point I am trying to make is that if you know where exactly you intend to get to, then there are a lot of things you will do differently. More importantly, if you know where you are heading, you will be in a better position to know the best way of getting there.

So the question I want to ask you is this: "*where exactly are you going? What is your final destination?*"

This is important because if you know your destination, then it will be easier to decide on the most effective method to get from where you are to where you want to be. If you know where you want to get to in life, after completing your tertiary studies, then you'll be asking yourself if the courses you are studying or have done are the best means for getting you to your destination.

So you need to seriously ask yourself: *where exactly am I going?* Having settled that, next, you need to try and form a picture of this destination because it is very likely that if you cannot visualize it in your mind, you will not likely know when you get there. Furthermore, having such a vision will serve as a strong motivator to keep you going, especially when things get tough.

I have often times asked students what plans they have for life after school and more often than not, I get the very quick-fire response, *"Oh, but the future is quite uncertain."*

Well, the truth is, it is not the future that is uncertain, it is the way you plan to walk into that future that is very certain. The certainty about the future is that it will come, just as night follows day. What is rather uncertain is whether or not you are ready for it. If you have accepted this reality that I am talking about and before you run off writing your dreams for the future, let me share a little secret with you:

You probably do not have a well thought out plan for the future after school, not because you forgot to plan or because you cannot write it, but it might be mainly because you do not yet have a dream. A dream, you might ask. Yes! You need a dream, a vision or an image of your future destination. This is totally different from your plan. You see, the plan is just the means of getting to the destination. For example, if you want to get to Madagascar in three days from London, you will assuredly know that driving, walking and running are not viable options for doing this. So here, your dream or destination is Madagascar, but the plan is the means you use to get there, which in this case would most likely be by plane. So you need a dream or vision to motivate you to act, and then the plan for attaining your dream.

The reason I am emphasizing the destination or dream or vision so much, comes from the recognition that for many students, the courses they choose, the school clubs they join, and the circle of friends they keep have absolutely no connection with their final destinations in life, and they realize this just too late. When this happens, most people lose the ability to bargain with life and so, find themselves having to settle for anything life has to offer them. In short, what I am saying is that if you have a destination/vision in mind, you will make decisions and choices based on the need to fulfil this dream or reach that destination, rather than on what you "*feel*" at the time.

I used to work for a peace-building organisation and

on a trip to a certain country for the first time; I took a taxi from the airport to my hotel. It must have been a journey of about fifteen minutes but cost me about tens of US dollars. I thought that this was a very expensive ride, but I told myself that this was one of those ridiculously expensive countries. On the day of my departure, I checked out of my hotel and asked the receptionist to call me a taxi to the airport. He looked at me perplexed and started laughing. When I asked him what the matter was, he got up and asked me to follow him to one of the main doors, opening into the garden area. He then pointed to the departure lounge of the airport which was right behind the hotel! I felt both stupid and amused at the discovery, realizing that I had paid some dollars for getting to a place I could have walked to.

The moral of the story is simple – because I did not know my destination, what it looked like, where it was located etc., I could not correctly figure out if the best way of getting there was by walking or by taking a taxi. So you see, the hotel was my destination or vision and the taxi or walking was the plan for getting there. But making a plan depended on knowing where I was going, when I needed to get there and in some cases, what I needed to be doing there.

The question again is – "*Where exactly are you*

headed?" What are the pictures you have about how you want your life to turn out? After university, you will find a job, marry, have children, then what? Are these your destinations?

I would suggest your destination or dream should be something you can leave behind, that makes the world better than you came to find it.

I will tell you why. Everything you see in this world and everything you will ever use or enjoy was once somebody's dream. This book you are reading is a small part of my destination and dream. The phone you use, that was someone's dream. Google, Apple, the hospitals, Facebook, you name it – everything that has made your life a little better to live, even the very independence of your country or its pillars of freedom and justice were someone's dream. \yes, the chocolate you so enjoy started off as a farmer's dream to be a producer of the best cocoa. Life is all about dreams, it is all about destinations.

I challenge you – with all the knowledge you have acquired or are still acquiring in school, DON'T go through life without dreams or without knowing your destination. You are worth more than that. You should leave your mark behind for the good of others.

If you are a student reading this book, then remember, you are the world. If you fail to have dreams and fulfil them, if you fail to get to your destination, the world is doomed. There is neither a race nor mind greater than yours, but you must have dreams or know your destination, in order to fulfil your potential.

When you have a dream, then it will make a lot more sense whether the best plan is to set up a business, find a job right after school, go look for greener pastures, take another course of study or just sit at home and allow life to take its course.

I want you to remember this – every day that passes by for which you have not done anything to move closer to your destination is you robbing the world of your gifts and talents and a chance for it to become a better place.

There are people out there who have achieved big dreams or reached unbelievable destinations with their lives without even a tenth of your education or knowledge. Surely, you can achieve much more!

3. *How Have You Been Wired?*
This question arises in respect of making career choices and trying to find out what the motivating factors are, for your field of study or endeavour. I will first tell you a story about my own family to illustrate the point I want to make.

I come from a family of four children - two brothers

and two sisters. Whilst we were children living with our father in Nigeria, I remember him buying us one of those huge colouring books showing different professions, one on each page. We were all so excited when he asked us to each take a turn with the book and colour which profession we wanted to be in when we grew up. My eldest sister coloured a banker, and I still remember my dad's face lighting up with a smile, accompanied by praises for her. The truth is she now works for a Central Bank. My other sister coloured an actress/dancer and I remember the first question my dad asked her in Ewe was "Etsu kum ne la? This literally translates from my local dialect into English as "Are you mad?" He was furious! I later overheard my mum saying to let the girl be what she strongly feels connected to, but my dad would have none of that – not his child. On hindsight, I genuinely think she would have been a big hit as an actress – and that is the truth. She is a professional beautician now.

It was my turn and I had a choice to please my father or follow my own true desires (and get screamed at). I went against the latter and I coloured an architect and a civil engineer. My father was delighted and praised me lavishly, after all, he himself was a civil engineer – he was over the moon. However, somewhere between sixth form and university, I recognized my error and made a U-turn to change directions. Today, I am a chartered certified accountant, a critical thinking trainer and an author because writing, creative thinking and being analytical are the three things I am wired to do - I can do them every day for the rest of my life and still love it.

The point I want to make is that many of us become what we are professionally, largely through external pressures. Just pause a moment and think carefully about the part some of the following factors played or are still playing in your choice of a career:

1. Pressure from family and close relationships;
2. The need to conform in order to belong;
3. Financial and monetary pressures; and
4. Pressure from frustrations in life.

If any part of your career-life is decided this way, there is a strong likelihood that you will be largely unfulfilled and most likely unsuccessful too. This is because if any of these pressures cease to exist, your fundamental motivation for choosing the related course of study or following a certain career is effectively gone. Looking at it from another perspective, if you are wired in a certain manner and are acting contrary to this by doing what you are naturally not good at, you are hardly likely to be happy doing it

If you ignore the advice I am about to give you, believe you me, you are likely to end up as one of those people who hate waking up in the morning and going to their job or who cannot wait for five o'clock in order to leave work (assuming all other aspects of your life are running well). Is this what you want to do for the rest of your life?

There is a way you can be both successful and happy in your career - assuming all other aspects of your life are sound. By the word successful, I do not only mean having a lot of money to spend, but also, making a lasting impact on others and experiencing a sense of satisfaction and fulfilment in one's career. In order to arrive at this destination, you will need to identify what you are naturally good at and get involved in a career that generally uses a lot of that natural acumen - not what others say you should be doing. If your career allows you to apply a lot more of your natural strengths, then work will become a source of immense pleasure even when the work demands are many. This is so because you will enjoy what you are doing – and it contributes immensely to your success and personal happiness.

To illustrate the point, let us consider the differences between a hair blow-dryer and a carpet vacuum cleaner. Almost all the electronic components found in these two gadgets are very much the same, but because they have been wired for different purposes they operate differently. The vacuum cleaner operates by a suction effect and the hair dryer by a blowing effect. To try to use either to do the task of the other would be disastrous, even so, it is with you when you are operating contrary to your natural wiring.

This is why it is important for you, when choosing a career, to know your wiring and let this guide you in your decision-making. Ask yourself again - *what comes to me naturally or – how am I wired?*

Yes, you may have studied and passed all your chemistry exams but are you really wired for work as a laboratory person? Similarly, you are studying for a career in architecture and civil engineering, but are you naturally able to quickly and mentally visualize images in 3-D? Persons who are naturally good at mathematics and who can visually but easily create 3-dimensional structures in their minds are more suited for careers in engineering or architecture just as those who are naturally good at analytical, logical and numerical reasoning are a good fit for computer programming, accounting and the like. So, it comes down to the same question – *what are you naturally good at?*

You may feel worried if you start comparing what you are good at and the path you are on now and realizing they are both out of sync. But calm your fears and take a few days to think about the possibility and impacts of changing paths at this moment in your life. Consider all options, weigh the implications of each, the costs and the benefits that could accrue. It might be scary, but if you acknowledge the truth about yourself, that a change needs to be made, then, have the courage to do so now, rather than live in regret later. Change is a part of life and even more so in our increasingly ever changing world.

It all comes down to this – the choice is yours and no one else's. Only you can be held responsible for whatever you become. For this reason you are being advised to let your decision regarding your lifetime career be guided by how you are naturally wired – your strengths.

Make no excuses; everyone is born wired in a very specific way – you just need to find out how and what this is for you. Examine yourself, ask close friends and relatives etc. but whatever you do – do not lie to yourself.

4.   *What Do You Know?*

The truth, even though unpleasant sometimes should never be allowed to be so unpleasant that it stops you making the necessary changes in life – so cheer up, as I tell you one of these hard truths. The good news is – you can do something about it.

Several years ago, the knowledge gained all the way up to a university bachelors or master's stage was almost sufficient to take one through the rest of their working life. For example, my father, since he became a building technologist has hardly had to add a lot more to the knowledge he had acquired to take him to the peak of his career and into retirement. Today, the situation has changed drastically. Information is currently growing at an exponential rate as several millions of research, thematic and other documents are published in print and electronically daily, weekly, monthly and annually. The effect of this information explosion is a demand for lifelong learning by everyone who hopes to remain relevant in the working world.

It is therefore a hard truth, that if you fail to supplement your formal education with regular ongoing learning, the shelf life of your knowledge acquired at university or college will be very short. In fact, by the time you complete a three-year tertiary education programme, the knowledge you acquired in the first year is likely to have become partially obsolete by the time you are ready to graduate.

For many people who now have a degree or professional qualifications or both, the question always arises – *"what is the extra edge you have to offer your employers?"* It requires continuous learning to be able to offer that extra value that employers are looking for. Formal information obtained within tertiary institutions is no longer sufficient. You must supplement this with knowledge through continuing education as well as by self-education.

The idea that all your learning must take place in a formal classroom has long become outdated. Today, it is not enough to merely listen to the news or simply read a magazine or a daily newspaper or spend a few hours on social media like Facebook and Twitter as a way of keeping abreast with the major things happening around the world. You also must learn to read purposefully which means that you target areas of your life to which you want to add value and find and read materials in these fields. Suffice it to say, one of the best and most rewarding investments anyone can make is to add value to themselves because it will lead to success in whatever endeavour you may find yourself.

If possible, maybe you can do what I do. I have made it a habit of attending at least two seminars each year- one in a field that is unfamiliar to me to widen my knowledge base; and the other to deepen an area in which I am already working.

Whatever you do, read widely on things that will add value to your life. The Chinese philosopher Confucius once said "*to know, is to know that you know nothing – that is the true meaning of knowledge.*" Also, Vernon Howard says: "*Always walk through life as if you have something new to learn, and you will.*"

I tell you the following to demonstrate a point about the benefit of reading compared to being ignorant. In England, I had a friend who once told me that he was going to start a property business soon. My curt response was, "*Oh that's good.*" He was not too pleased with my short answer so he asked me if that was all I was going to say. I told him no, but that he would not like what I had to say. He insisted that I tell him and so I asked him, "*How much have you read on British property taxation?*" His immediate response was that he was going into property not taxation. Then I said to him: "*Well you see, I am an accountant and I know that the UK taxation regime alone can wipe off close to 65% of your profits from property if you don't manage it properly.*"

You'll be happy to know (sarcastically speaking) that my friend never said a word again for the rest of the evening. I had given him the benefit of my insight – but he chose to wish his investments in the air instead of reading.

In the world we live in today, there is hardly anything that you want to do that someone has not already done and or written about. The same can be said about mistakes - there is hardly any that you are about to make that someone has not already made and or written about it. Reading books – print or electronic – provides an essential roadmap and prevents highly unnecessary accidents of life. Readers will always lead the unread.

May I ask: How many value-adding books you've read in the last one month, six months or a year? Right! *Here's the deal – every single month you walk around without adding any value to yourself, in terms of knowledge, equals six months into your future that you have prepared to fail.*

The message is clear. Start reading something now. If you have a dream, a vision or an idea of how you want your life to turn out, there are plenty of ordinary as well as great men and women who have travelled those paths already. Please buy a value-adding book and start reading. You may at least learn about the mistakes many have made so you will not make the same. You can also be inspired by what they do and be further motivated to achieve your dream.

What you know, is what you can become – so start reading something now!

5. *What Do You Spend Your Time Thinking About?*
In the Bible, Proverbs 23:7 tells us that "*as a man thinks, so is he*" – and there is much truth in that statement.

When you look around, you might begin to notice that most things we used to do as humans are becoming automated and sadly, our thinking is going down the same path. The computer has taken over many of our brain activities such as calculating and remembering things. The consequences of we allowing computers to think for is that our minds are hardly trained these days to think deliberately and continuously. You might wish to refute this, but let us stop for a minute and do a very small, but honest, exercise.

Has it ever occurred to you that some of the few times we've really sat down to think and formulate deliberate actions that would leap our lives and/or those of others forward are:

1. When we have a serious need;
2. When there is a problem that demands a solution and
3. When we are in fear.

Most people would rarely set aside any time to just think consciously about their lives and what impacts they can make to humanity and the world at large. Yes, we might occasionally do some quick thinking, but rarely do we deliberately take time to think, with the intent of arriving at solutions beneficial to self and wider society.

I have an interesting habit of waking up most days in the week at about 03.30 a.m. to think. I just sit there in a comfortable sofa and ask myself: what products or services can I create out of my achievements, education and experiences, to benefit others? What are the needs of people around me that I can satisfy? Do I have a problem that many other people have, can I find a solution to it, and, if so, will it be an applicable solution for the many other people with the same problem?

So why am I encouraging you to make thinking a conscious and proactive endeavour rather than making it reactive? Because I have observed that the people who become exceptionally successful in life are those who are in the primary business of satisfying other people's needs. For them to do this effectively, they must have spent quite some time thinking when many others weren't. I do not know what you have or are studying, but you need to start thinking how you can use your skills and talents to satisfy the needs of larger society or to solve problems faced by many. And here's the best part – if you can find an anticipated solution to people's problem before it even becomes a need, the world will be at your feet.

Let us look at Facebook as an example. The billions of people who currently use it have always had a need for social interaction. Mark Zuckerberg, the owner of

Facebook, did not create that need; neither did he create the desire of billions of people over the world to use the internet – the internet already existed too. All Mark did was to provide people with a solution to the problem of needing to combine their natural desire for social interaction and the necessity to use the internet. Similarly, Thomas Edison, famous for inventing the light bulb (although disputed in some quarters), sat down to think consciously about inventing a bulb, not from any pressure or fear – he simply allowed thinking to take its natural course; eventually, the light bulb emerged. This would not have happened if he had not devoted time to thinking.

You have to begin to make time to think consciously. I always recommend that you keep a small book of thoughts and to get into the habit of writing down even the craziest thing that comes into your mind. You need not worry if people say it is a crazy idea. Yes, it is crazy to them because it is not their idea. I will paraphrase what my favourite iron lady, Margaret Thatcher, once said: *"if I do what is right, people will talk and if I do what is wrong, people will still talk, so I'll just do what I believe in and let those that want to talk, talk."* So ignore the commentaries of spectators and go on to make your dent on the world, through your thinking.

Think. And when you are done thinking, think again

some more. If you think enough, you will soon start stepping into the future, before many other people get there.

Perhaps, it is worth concluding this section by bringing to your attention that school generally only teaches you **what to think**. You will have to take it on yourself to learn **how to think** because that's what you will need to make life work for you. Learning how to think helps you create your world and one for others, while just learning what to think only helps you live other people's lives through their theories and philosophies.

Think! Think! Think!

6. *Are You A Creative Thinker In A Highly Creative World?*

Thinking as we saw above is an excellent and rewarding endeavour – but only when it can generate creative and lasting solutions to problems. It requires thinking to be creative, in that it helps evolve smart solutions for old and new problems alike.

So why should being creative matter to you, anyway? Well, as we mentioned in the beginning of this book, the world is filled with problems, each problem, presenting an opportunity waiting to be explored by those brave enough to attempt offering the right solution. This calls for creativity. Today, an abundance of information is readily available but the challenge is how to effectively apply it to problem-solving. This is where creativity comes in – when someone is able to bring together previously disconnected ideas and fuse them in non-traditional ways to produce something new. This kind of thinking is what distinguishes the leaders from the followers and the extraordinary from the ordinary. Becoming a creative thinker – doing things in a way others have not yet imagined- is one sure way to gain the competitive edge in the world of work after you leave tertiary school.

Unfortunately, not many people are given to thinking creatively – it comes naturally for some, but can equally be learned by others. This is good news for those of us who are not naturally endowed in this area. Yes, you can learn to think in a manner that will consistently generate creative solutions – that is one of the hallmarks of creativity.

I will now summarily introduce you to three such techniques that you can employ to consistently generate creative ideas and solutions to problems of any kind:

(i). Round Holes Looking for Round Pegs: More often than not, because of how our minds have been programmed over time, one automatically tends to think every problem requires a brand new solution. Truth is, sometimes there are solutions that have

been found in other areas, but are equally usable for problems in newer areas. In other words, these are already existing solutions floating around looking for new problems to solve.

For example, there is a thermostat, used to control the temperature of the electric iron, whereby, the iron automatically stops heating when it gets to a set temperature and vice versa. This same technology has now been applied to temperature control in modern cars where you can programme the temperature you want in your car, depending on who is driving it - and the system ensures that it is maintained by turning off the air-conditioner whenever the desired temperature is reached. This exemplifies creativity where an old solution taken from elsewhere is applied in a new way in a totally different setting – originally applied in heat, now re-applied in cold temperature control.

(ii) Reverse, Inverse, Flip, and Switch: Sometimes re-arranging a problem or an already existing solution in a different order can by itself become a creative solution to a problem. That is exactly how the telephone call back service was invented. Under normal circumstances, you would pick up a phone, call a company and stay on the line for minutes on

end before you get an answer and you had to pay for the call. With the new call-back service, you can now call a company and if they are busy, you simply dial *67 (depending on your country and service provider) and hang up. When their line is less busy, their phone system calls you back automatically and they pay for the bill, not you. It is like having a personal secretary to keep trying someone's number until they get through to them and then transfer the connected call to your office. The only exception is that this time around, the company you are trying to reach pays the bill. This is another example of creativity expressed by simply reversing the normal order.

(iii) The Adam and Eve: Finally, this is what I call the "Adam & Eve" creative thinking mechanism. In the Holy Bible, specifically in Genesis, we are made aware Adam and Eve are actually one and sometimes, this is exactly one of the ways in which creativity can be sparked. Sometimes, all it takes is for someone, in trying to solve a problem, to bring together two different stand-alone items, actions, etc. which when combined, evolve an entirely new and creative solution. The mirror approach to this is to split a product or an already existing solution into differ-

ent components which could also generate a totally new creative solution. Again, let us take Facebook as an example where none of the components were totally new. Before Facebook, there was the internet and the various platforms used separately to upload photos and to send and receive messages and other types of texts. In addition, there was already a God-given need for human beings to communicate with each other as social beings. What Mark Zuckerman did was to combine all these features in a creative manner and thereby, developed what is known today as Facebook.

So hopefully, you now have some techniques with which you can apply creative thinking straightaway. The ability to think creatively and come up with new solutions is applicable in every area of life and I can assure you that this ability will give you a competitive edge wherever you choose to apply it.

In today's world, creative thinking is an extremely important currency that determines the leaders of the pack in any industry and the followers in the same – possessing such a skill makes whatever you do highly valued and well rewarded.

Remember, don't only think – think creatively.

7. *Do You Know Where the World Is Headed?*

Imagine a heavy-duty haulage truck travelling at 121 Mph and a small saloon car also traveling at 100 Mph. There are two scenarios I want you to envision. In scenario one, imagine the two vehicles are driving on the same single lane road but in opposite directions, facing each other. In scenario two, both the truck and the small saloon car are driving in the same direction, the small one following behind the big one. Now, tell me, in which scenario there is likely to be a crash and which of the vehicles is most likely to sustain the most damage?

That truck in the scenario is the world and the little saloon car, is you. This sounds frightening, does it not? What I wish to highlight in this section is a few of the directions in which the world is moving in order to help you choose whether you want to be going in the same direction the world is flowing or to go against it. I think it is important that you know this, because it is hardly likely that you will be told this in school, prior to graduation. Here are my tips for you:

1. The first thing you need to know is that the world is speeding up. By this, I mean everything is happening faster. Technology is evolving faster than we can imagine; decision- making now needs to be done in a much shorter

time; systems and people are integrating at a much faster pace; physical and man-made barriers of the world are disappearing fast; and previously held consumer behaviours, such as brand loyalty, are almost non-existent in today's world with a multiplicity of buying options. Information is becoming available at a faster rate than ever before and in the workplace, better and faster ways are being found to achieve greater, higher quality outputs and outcomes than yester year.

In an increasingly faster world therefore, you have to consciously find ways of keeping abreast of the accompanying opportunities, challenges, competition and risks. As a result of all of these major shifts in the world's operating pace, you as an individual who wishes to standout and survive in our world will not only need to learn how to work faster, but smarter – if you ignore this trend and walk in the opposite direction to the world (by being slower), you may get crashed out.

2. The world is becoming more seamlessly integrated, hence, more complex and, hopefully, more efficient. For example, the technologies used to perform individual tasks are now integrated to do multiple activities leading to greater efficiency. To prove this, all you have to do is to consider your mobile phone. Besides being a phone, it

is now a camera, a clock, a voice recorder, an email connection, a photo album and it can do a myriad of others things by using the various available applications. Years ago, all of those were done by separate equipment with their own capabilities.

This is no longer the case with integrated technology which seeks to increase efficiency and provide new competitive advantages. On a personal level, you must understand that you not only need to keep abreast with evolving technology that will help you achieve greater efficiency in shorter timeframes, but you also need to realize that some degree of integration on your part is also necessary if you wish to be successful in your career. This has to do with what you are studying for the world of work. For example, it is no longer enough to have just studied pharmacy in order to become a pharmacist, but you will also need to incorporate courses on information technology and business management into your programme in order to be better able to manage a pharmacy. This is the way of the integrated world in which we now find ourselves – if you ignore this trend and walk in the opposite direction to the world (by not synchronising activities, operations and themes that you currently do separately), you may get crashed out.

3. Markets are not just physical anymore; they are also in cyberspace as more and more sales are transacted using the internet. This, therefore, means that you cannot continue thinking of the market place as being confined within four walls or national borders. Everybody in the world is equally a customer, supplier, employee and employer. The entire world has suddenly become our stage for both competition and opportunity, not just our domestic economies.

So whereas you would have originally thought that after school, you will be competing with only the half a million other unemployed persons in your country, in fact, this is no longer the case. Since the world is now a global marketplace due to technology, your employment prospects after school are going to possibly be in competition with the unemployed thousands in your local economy, plus the thousands and perhaps millions of freelance workers from all over the world who work through websites such as Odesk, Peopleperhour and Fiverr.

The ability to work from remote locations via technology has expanded the access of local employers to a global workforce, enabling employers to get their work done by persons not physically present in their own country. With this kind of scenario, suddenly, you realize that the contents of your courses of study must also equip you to compete in the global marketplace.

This knowledge should force you to recognize that the workplace is changing drastically and you have to start thinking globally – if you ignore this trend and walk in the opposite direction to the world (by ill-equipping yourself to compete globally), you may get crashed out.

CONCLUSION

The American philosopher, Elbert Hubbard, once said *"The greatest mistake you can make in life is to continually be afraid to make one because in denying to make mistakes and fail, you are also denying to try and succeed."*

My intent is by no means to scare you about the world that awaits you outside your tertiary education; it is my sincere hope that through this book, you will come face to face with and grasp some of the realities that await you out there and be prepared for them before you graduate.

The knowledge and understanding gleaned from this book should help not only prepare you, but also give you a competitive advantage over other graduates. For this reason, you need to spend some time reading and mulling over the contents of this book more than once and hopefully, you will begin to see the world in a light that allows you to position yourself strategically for success.

Wherever your journey after graduation takes you, I wish you the very best of success in your endeavours – I believe you will succeed!

AUTHOR'S OTHER WORKS

Title:	Is This Why Africa Is? (E-book & Paperback)
Description:	I ask all the questions about Africa that nobody else will. Deep, profound questions
Availability:	Amazon & Kindle
Link to View:	http://goo.gl/ecRMig

Title:	Where Did God Hide His Diamonds? (E-book & Paperback)
Description:	Discovering what exactly God has hidden in you, finding it & prospering freely from it
Availability:	Amazon & Kindle
Link to View:	http://goo.gl/ecRMig

Title:	Doing Business with God (E-book & Paperback)
Description:	60 shocking biblical principles for extraordinary leadership, business and politics.
Availability:	Amazon & Kindle
Link to View:	http://goo.gl/ecRMig

Title:	Midnight Philosophies (E-book & Paperback)
Description:	My Deep thoughts, Philosophies, Reflections – Whispers of my mind.

Availability:	Amazon & Kindle
Link to View:	http://goo.gl/ecRMig

Title:	This Godly Child of Mine (E-book & Paperback)
Description:	A revelatory book on how to raise godly children in a perverse and lawless world
Availability:	Amazon & Kindle
Link to View:	http://goo.gl/ecRMig

Title:	The Deputy Minister for Corruption (E-book & Paperback)
Description:	A Novel
Availability:	Amazon & Kindle
Link to View:	http://goo.gl/ecRMig

Title:	A Dove in the Storm (E-book & Paperback)
Description:	A Novel
Availability:	Amazon & Kindle
Link to View:	http://goo.gl/ecRMig

Title:	100% JOB INTERVIEW SUCCESS (E-book & Paperback)
Description:	A simple, straightforward guide to passing every job interview you attend.
Availability:	Amazon & Kindle
Link to View:	http://goo.gl/ecRMig

Title:	Bible-by-Heart (Mobile App)
Description:	A simple but effective App to help anyone memorize 500 Bible verses in a year.
Availability:	iTunes & Google Play Stores
Link to View:	http://goo.gl/T3UdPN (i-Tunes)
Link to View:	http://goo.gl/ljnECR (Android)

Title:	Holy Rat (Mobile Game)
Description:	An exciting Christian mobile game that unwittingly gets you addicted to the word.
Availability:	iTunes & Google Play Stores
Link to View:	http://goo.gl/bygjBi (i-Tunes)
Link to View:	http://goo.gl/F18RM0 (Android)

ABOUT THE AUTHOR

Marricke Kofi Gane, is a gifted African Author, Philosopher, Public Speaker, Coach and Educationist. His writings carry real depth, are highly motivating yet challenging every status quo. He displays dexterity of mind and refined humour where appropriate. He is never shy in some of his works, to show a strong balance between his Christian roots and the reality of living in today's world.

Discover for yourself, all that his writings stand for - to dare, to motivate, to impact!! For more on him, visit:

www.marrickekofigane.com

Dear Reader,

Thank you for reading this book. I am hopeful that the information provided in it has given you some new learning, challenged you, or provided some answers and inspiration.

I respectfully ask your indulgence in 2 simple ways:

1. Whatever positive action(s) this book has inspired you to take, DO IT NOW. Not later.

2. Help other potential readers who without you, may never read this book by simply following the link below to leave a review. It only takes 3 minutes, but it could be a lifetime blessing for someone out there.

http://goo.gl/v03bu2

Thank you once again for everything

Marricke Kofi GANE

www.ingramcontent.com/pod-product-compliance
Lightning Source LLC
Chambersburg PA
CBHW060522280326
41933CB00014B/3075